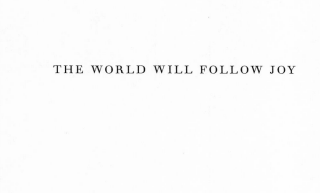

THE WORLD WILL FOLLOW JOY

THE
WORLD
WILL
FOLLOW
JOY

*Turning Madness
into Flowers*

{ New Poems }

ALICE WALKER

THE NEW PRESS
NEW YORK

Requests for permission to reproduce selections from this book
should be mailed to: Permissions Department, The New Press,
38 Greene Street, New York, NY 10013.

Published in the United States by
The New Press, New York, 2013
Distributed by Perseus Distribution

LIBRARY OF CONGRESS CATALOGING-IN-PUBLICATION DATA
Walker, Alice, 1944-
  [Poems. Selections]
  The world will follow joy : turning madness into flowers (new
poems) / Alice Walker.
    pages cm
  Poems.
  ISBN 978-1-59558-876-0 (hardcover) —
  ISBN 978-1-59558-887-6 (e-book) (print)
  I. Title.
  PS3573.A425W67 2013
  811'.54—dc23   2012041853

The New Press publishes books that promote and enrich
public discussion and understanding of the issues vital to our
democracy and to a more equitable world. These books are
made possible by the enthusiasm of our readers; the support of
a committed group of donors, large and small; the collaboration
of our many partners in the independent media and the not-for-
profit sector; booksellers, who often hand-sell New Press books;
librarians; and above all by our authors.

www.thenewpress.com

Book design by Lovedog Studio
This book was set in Monotype Walbaum

Printed in the United States of America

10 9 8 7 6 5 4 3 2 1

Contents

In loving memory of Rudolph Byrd
so deeply missed
and of the miracle that was our trust.

And for G. Kaleo Larson
My working-class hero.

Foreword

> *To a woman in whom the state of true*
> *motherhood has awakened, all creatures*
> *are her children. This love, this mother-*
> *hood, is Divine Love—and that is God.*
>
> *—Amma*

Turning Madness into Flowers

It is my thought that the ugliness of war, of gratuitous violence in all its hideous forms, will cease very soon to appeal to even the most insulated of human beings. It will be seen by all for what it is: a threat to our well-being, to our survival as a species, and to our happiness. The brutal murder of our common mother, while we look on like frightened children, will become an unbearable visceral suffering that we will refuse to bear. We will abandon the way of the saw, the jackhammer and the drill. Of bombs, too.

As religions and philosophies that espouse or excuse violence reveal their true poverty of hope for humankind, there will be a great awakening, already begun, about what is of value in life.

We will turn our madness into flowers as a way of moving completely beyond all previous and current programming of how we must toe the familiar line of submission and fear, following orders given us by miserable souls who, somehow, have managed to almost completely control us. We will discover something wonderful: that the world really does not enjoy following the dictates of sociopaths and psychopaths, those who treat the earth, our mother, as if she is wrong, and must be constantly corrected, in as sadistic and domineering a way as that of a drunken husband who kills his wife.

The world—the animals, including us humans—wants to be engaged in something entirely other, seeing, and delighting in, the stark wonder of where we are: This place. This gift. This paradise.

We want to follow joy.

And we shall.

The madness, of course, for each one of us, will have to be sorted out. [1]

—*Alice Walker*
August 2012
www.AliceWalkersGarden.com

What Makes the Dalai Lama Lovable?

His posture
From so many years
Holding his robe with one hand
Is odd.

His gait
Also.

One's own body
Aches
Witnessing
The sloping
Shoulders
& Angled
Neck;

One hopes
He
Attends
Yoga class
Or does Yoga
On his own

As part
Of prayer.

He smiles
As he bows
To Everything:
Accepting
The heavy
Burdens
Of
This earth;

Its
Toxic
Evils
& Prolific
Insults.

Even so,
He sleeps
Through
The night
Like a child
Because
Thank goodness
That is something

Else
Daylong
Meditation
Assures.

You could cry
Yourself to sleep
On his behalf
& He
Has done that
Too.

Life
Has been
A great
Endless
Tearing away
For
Him.

From
Mother, Father, Siblings, Country, Home.
And yet
Clearly
His mother
Loved him;

His brother & sister
Too: Even his
Not so constant father,
Who
When Tenzin was
A boy
Shared
With him
Delicious
Scraps
Of
Succulent
Pork.

He laughs
Telling this
Story
Over half a century
Later
&
To who knows
How many
Puzzled
Vegetarians:
About
The way he sat

Behind

His father's chair

Like a dog,

Relishing

Each juicy

Greasy

Bite.

Whenever I see

The Dalai Lama

My first impulse

Is to laugh

I am so happy

To

Lay eyes

On

One

So effortlessly

Beautiful.

That balding head

That holds

A shine;

Those wire framed

Glasses

That might

Have come

From
Anywhere.

That look of having offered
All he has.
He is my teacher;
Just staying alive.
Other teachers
I have had
Resemble him
In some way;

They too
Were
&
Are
Smart
And Humble;
Fascinated
By Science & things like
Time,
Eternity,
Cause & Effect;
The Evolution
Of the Soul.

A
Soul
That
Might
Or might not
Exist.

They too
See all of us
—Banker, murderer, gardener, thief—
When they look
Out across
The world:

But that is not all
They see.

They see our suffering;
Our striving
To find
The right path;
The one with heart
We may only
Have heard about.

The Dalai Lama is Cool

A modern word
For
"Divine"
Because he wants
Only
Our collective
Health
& Happiness.

That's it!

What makes
Him
Lovable
Is
His holiness.

* * *

If I Was President ("Were" May Be Substituted by Those Who Prefer It)

If I was President
The first thing I would do
is call Mumia Abu-Jamal.
No,
if I was President
the first thing I would do
is call Leonard Peltier.
No,
if I was President
the first person I would call
is that rascal
John Trudell.
No,
the first person I'd call
is that other rascal
Dennis Banks.

I would also call
Alice Walker.

I would make a conference call.

And I would say this:

Yo, you troublemakers,
it is time to let all of us
out of prison.
Pack up your things.

Dennis and John,
collect Alice Walker
if you can find her:
in Mendocino, Molokai, Mexico or
Gaza,
& head out to the prisons
where Mumia and Leonard
are waiting for you.
They will be traveling
light.
Mumia used to own a lot
of papers
but they took most of those
away from him.
Leonard
will probably want to drag along
some of his
canvases.

Alice
who may well be
shopping
in New Delhi
will no doubt want to
dress up for the occasion
in a sparkly shalwar kemeez.

My next call is going to be
to the Cubans
all five of them;
so stop worrying.
For now, you're my fish.
I just had this long letter
from Alice and she has begged me
to put an end
to her suffering.

What? she said.
You think these men are the only ones who
    suffer
when Old Style America locks them up
& throws away
the key?
I can't tell you, she goes on,

the changes
this viciousness
has put me through,
and I have had a child to raise
& classes to teach
& food to buy
and just because
I'm a poet
it doesn't mean
I don't have to
pay the mortgage
or the rent.

Yet all these years,
nearly thirty or something
of them
I have been running around
the country
and the world
trying to arouse justice
for these men.
Tonsillitis
hasn't stopped me.
Migraine
hasn't stopped me.

Lyme disease
hasn't stopped me.
And why?
Because
knowing the country
that I'm in,
as you are destined to learn
it too,
I know wrong
when I see it.
If that chair you're sitting in
could speak
you would have it moved
to another room.
You would burn it.

So, amigos,
pack your things.
Alice and John and Dennis
are on their way.
They are bringing prayers from Nilak Butler
    and Bill Wahpepah;
they are bringing sweet grass and white sage
from Pine Ridge.

I am the President
at least until the Corporations
purchase the next election,
and this is what I choose
to do on my first day.[2]

* * *

From: Poems for My Girls

The Chicken Chronicles: Sitting with
the Angels Who Have Returned with
My Memories
—*Pax Ameracauna*, chapter 22

How can Humanity
look the deer
in
the face?
How can I,
having erected
my fence?

*   *   *

Don't be like those who ask for everything

For Queen Miriam (Makeba) who stood on
swollen feet and sang her people to freedom

Don't be like those who ask for everything:
praise, a blurb, a free ride in my rented
limousine. They ask for everything but never
    offer
anything in return.
Be like those who can see that my feet ache
from across a crowded room
that a foot rub
if I'm agreeable
never mind the staring
is the best way to smile
& say hello
to me.

* * *

Knowing You Might
Someday Come

For Kaleo

Knowing you might someday come

and how unprepared I've always

been

like Mr. Sloppy

in Charles Dickens'

our Mutual Friend

I made a list:

not meat, vegetables, beer and pudding

but number l, warmth.

number 2, warmth.

number 3, warmth.

number 4, a good snuggler.

number 5, someone who sings

while he/she works.

number 6, a dancer.

number 7, someone who grows

& is intrigued by

the mind. And

by the spirit too.

Number 8, someone who is loved

by animals; and loves
them back without
a thought.
number 9, someone who smells
delicious.
number 10, someone whose anger
lasts no longer than mine.
number 11, someone who
stands beside me. behind me. If necessary
in front of me.
number 12, someone who
is a passable cook.
number 13, Someone who laughs
a lot, thinks I have a fine
sense
of humor
& has friends.
number 14, someone who can be
original in dress:
stylish
warlock—in silver, lapis
& black—to my witch.

* * *

Turning Madness into Flowers #1

If my sorrow were deeper
I'd be, along with you, under
the ocean's floor;
but today I learn that the oil
that pools beneath the ocean floor
is essence
residue
remains
of all our
relations
all
our ancestors who have died and turned to oil
without our witness
eons ago.
We've always belonged to them.
Speaking for you, hanging, weeping, over the
    water's edge
as well as for myself.
It is our grief
heavy, relentless,
trudging
us, however resistant,

to the decaying and rotten
bottom of things:
our grief bringing
us home.

*   *   *

What It Feels Like

As if I've swallowed
A watermelon
And
Sidestepping
My digestive tract
It has lodged
In my heart.
There it lies
Green
& whole
with a luscious
red
heart of its own
daring me
to cut.

*   *   *

Before I Leave the Stage

Before I leave the stage
I will sing the only song
I was meant truly to sing.

It is the song
of I AM.
Yes: I am Me
&
You.
WE ARE.

I love Us with every drop
of our blood
every atom of our cells
our waving particles
—undaunted flags of our Being—
neither here nor there.

* * *

Remember?

Remember
When we ended
It all
—for a weekend—
& how
We knew?
You took
The tea bowl
That I
Broke
In
Carelessness
To glue together
Again
At your
House.

* * *

Working Class Hero

My brothers knew
The things you know.
I did not scorn
learning them;
It's just my mind
Was busy being trained

For "Other Things":

Poetry, Philosophy, Literature.
Survival, for a girl.

But now,
What a relief
To see you understand
The ways
Of horses
Their shyness
& hatred
Of
Loneliness:

That you will not
Hesitate
To rescue
An old horse,
Dying on
His feet
&
That you will
Cheerfully
Wash him,
Aged
&
Incontinent
Head
To
Toe. Missing
With your bucket
&
Rag
Not
One
Hidden
Crevice
As he
Trembles
& weeps.

What peace
To see
Raising chickens
Does not
Mystify you
and
Hot water heaters
& their ways
Are well known;
That electricity
& how it
Works
Is something
Within
Your grasp.

That you can
Get a car
To run
By poking
It in
A few mysterious
Places
Under
The hood.

That you can

Fix a

Broken

Anything: battery, truck, stove,

Door, fridge, lamp, chicken coop hinge

While teaching me

The ins and outs

Of Opera

Or

While singing

Lusty

Italian

Tenor

That

Shakes

The walls.

That you can

Sit, comfy,

Unperturbed

By traffic

In the womb-like

Back seat

Of my

Aging

Chariot

While I drive

& you

Ride

The silver

Black

& Golden

Horses

Of

Your

Trumpet.

* * *

The Ways of Water

With your unknown
to me
Odd magic
You came
To me:
Your truck
Backfiring
As if sending
Out
Rockets
To the
Stars

You came
In
So gracefully
Rockets
Silenced
Behind you &
Set
To work
As if nothing
Brought you

Greater

Joy.

I did not see Life was

About to change, as it does,

When odd magic appears:

There was

No music

Yet.

Chatting

About relationships, our freedom

From same,

Which we

So defended;

About water, faucet

Drips;

The gifts

Of growing older;

You set to work

& I, standing above you

As you lay on

Your back

Studied

Your feet:

Well cared for

In ocean blue
Sandals
Made of tough
Plastic.

Buddies,
We said, we agreed
That's what we
Needed.
How about going out
Together as buddies
For a night of music
& dance? My first
Indication
That song
Had a place
In
Your world.

Two years later
The leak
In my kitchen
Sink
Remains
Fixed
As well as

The leak
I never mentioned
In my spirit.

Early and late
We savor
The music
That comes
From
Your horn
The Golden Phoenix
That travels
With us
Everywhere

Your sound
Your love of Miles & Bird
& Wynton
Making
Friends of strangers
Around
The globe.

In Poor
Countries
Where

The grass

Has died

& the ponies

& oxen

Also

& the people

Have nothing

To bathe in

Or to drink &

Yet are soothed

By your cool

& liquid

Music, which

You pour over them

So freely,

I want to tell them:

Yes, he is also

A water man.

Yes, he also knows

The ways

Of water.

But they know this.

* * *

You Want to Grow Old Like the Carters

For Jimmy and Rosalynn Carter
of Plains, Georgia

Let other leaders
Retire
To play golf
& write
Memoirs
About bombing
Villages
They've never seen.

Growing old
Presents a peril
They may not
Expect.

It is to lose
One's soul
In trivia
& irrelevance

The nerve
Endings
Blunted
By the constant
Pressure
Of moral
Indifference.

Growing old
A curse:
Not even
Generally speaking
Able
To relate
To whoever
Shares
Your house. Not the mansion
You inhabit
On the
Lovely stolen hill
Above the sea
Or the interior one:
The darkened
Desolate
Shack.

You want to grow old
Like
The Carters;
Curing blindness
&
Building houses
For
The Poor;

Making friends of those
Who believe
They must fight.

You want to grow old
Like
The Carters
Holding hands
With someone
You love
&
Riding bicycles
Leisurely
Where the ground
Is well known

& perfectly
Flat.

You want to find
And keep to the path
Laid down
Inside you
Such a long time
Ago.

You want to grow old
Like
The Carters:
Serene. Eyes
Twinkling
To be accused
Of
Not getting
It right.

Upfront, upright.
Speaking what to you is true.
A person rich in Mothers.
Beloved.

And:

Honoring what is black
In you.

* * *

The answer is: Live happily!

To all my relations who have known this
suffering.
And for Miles Davis, just because.
Happy New Year.

When you thought me poor,
my poverty was shaming.
When blackness was unwelcome
we found it best
that I stay home.

When by the miracle
of fierce dreaming and hard work
Life fulfilled our every want
you found me crassly
well off;
not trimly,
inconspicuously wealthy
like your rich friends.

Still black too,
Now

I owned too much and too many
of everything.

Woe is me: I became a
success! Blackness, who
knows how?
Became suddenly
in!

What to do?
Now that Fate appears
(for the moment anyhow)
to have dismissed
abject failure
in any case?
Now that moonlight and night
have blessed me.
Now that the sun
unaffected by criticism
of any sort,
implacably beams
the kiss-filled magic that creates
the dark and radiant wonder
of my face.

*   *   *

Word reaches us

For Congresswoman Gabrielle Giffords

Word reaches us
that you are sleeping, sleeping.
Dismayed
we have turned to the sea.
We encounter among others
walking there
a sense of what we have lost:
the broad expanse of humanity's
sensitivity to the oneness of itself.
Gabrielle,
while you sleep, resting your nimble
brain, we think of walking with you
in the valley
of the shadow of death; holding
you up.
We hope you can feel our grief;
our sorrow vast
like the ocean that draws us.
We know in this moment you teach us many
things:
how all across the world

there is no one who deserves this fate.
We know we must bleach and sterilize our
tongues,
brighten with understanding
all our dark thoughts.
Sister, whom I never met
except in this pain that has so
wounded you
thank you for reminding us
through your suffering
and your suspenseful sleep
that we must change.

*   *   *

When You See Water

When you see water in a stream
you say: oh, this is stream
water;
When you see water in the river
you say: oh, this is water
of the river;
When you see ocean
Water
you say: This is the ocean's
water!
But actually water is always
only itself
and does not belong
to any of these containers
though it creates them.
And so it is with you.

*   *   *

This is a story of how love works

This is the house for orphaned young girls;
the house that love built.

These are two of the beautiful girls who
will live there.

Here is a flower for them!

It all started without a beginning! How cool.
Alice was eating in a vegan restaurant
because she is always trying to do things
that sometimes she keeps failing at:
still, she was there, eating her greens and peas
and sweet potatoes. It was all really good!
There was a young woman seated near her
with a slender, elegant East African
body and super long locks
and this woman gave her a card that read:
Beautiful Loks!
There was a picture of a child gently touching
his mother's locks. Alice liked this because one
of her favorite things is tenderness!
Years went by. She and the young Kenyan
became friends. Over hair, actually.
And learning new things, like: Irish Moss.
Didn't Bob Marley swear by it? But what was
it? Exactly?

The Kenyan knew! Ground some up for
Alice. Watched her drink it, along with other
slippery stuff.

Her name is Mo'raa M.B., which Alice liked
the sound of. Her mother had died and her

aunt Kwamboka Okari raised her. Raised her really well, too; Alice was happy to see. She worked hard, always learning new things. She said Please, May I help you, Auntie, and best of all: Thank you.

When Alice looked around to find an orphanage to adopt, Mo'raa M.B. invited her aunt Kwamboka to Alice's for dinner (she was visiting the country). Kwamboka brought Alice a beautiful sculpture of a woman carrying a child on her back. They became friends.

Kwamboka with help from wonderful folks in the United States was running an orphanage for children in Kenya who'd lost their parents to AIDS.

Over the next two or three years the school at the orphanage needed many things that Alice was able to help with. A floor, books, uniforms, things like that. But then, Alice was given a magical gift by Yoko Ono; a gift so magical it would only work if it were immediately handed to someone else! Alice

loved this; and of course she always loved
Yoko Ono.

What did this mean?

The dormitory for girls was going up brick
by brick, with love and contributions of all
sizes flowing or creeping in! More and more
children, boys and girls, were finding their
way to the orphanage.

With Yoko Ono's offering, and in spiritual
cahoots with John Lennon, the girls'
dormitory was finished!

This is the house that love built. Let's look at
it again!

Red! What joy! Blue! Yes!

Alice feels happy every time she looks at these pictures sent by Kwamboka Okari (founder of the Margaret Okari Foundation's school and orphanage), of the girls Yvonne and Brenda, and of the cheerful residence the girls will occupy.

It is beautiful, just as housing for all our girls and boys should be. Wherever they are on the globe. (No child anywhere should live in ugly housing! Ugly housing damages the spirit. Not to mention the beauty-loving soul!)

When something wonderful like this happens, when friends connect regardless of being dead (some of them) or far away (others of them), we know we are on the right path. Thorns may still prick our feet as we trudge hopefully along, but there will be moments of sheer incandescent joy.

As, for instance, when Alice found herself face to face with someone she had loved long before he was born.
I have loved you since way before you were born,

she said to him.

He looked skeptical.

He was dressed like a handsome bumble bee
and this made Alice happy
because she loves bees.

They are the reason everything happens
thinks the farmer and flower grower in her
heart.

How can that be? He finally asked.

Simple, she said to him:

It is because I loved your parents.

When the world learned that you were
coming
some thirty-five years ago
I said a special prayer for you:
for your safety, for balance in life,
for your health and happiness.

Really? he said.

Really, she said.

And now, look at you:
a young man still,
but wise and thoughtful.

Someone who can talk sensibly
with someone twice your age.

And a woman, too!

You are well raised. Alice continued.

All of my prayers
seem to have been answered.
Thank you. He said.
They talked for a long time
and
amazing to Alice
it was as if she'd stumbled upon a wise
old man
from the mountains:
he had much to tell her, much to share
about the austerities and the benefits of grief.
She was enchanted. She was restored.
She was so happy
it was almost more
than she could stand.
This solace of love and understanding
that could become a resting place
for the sorrow in her own heart
over something rare
that she had lost in her own life
that somehow complemented
something and someone he lost
while still a child;
something
that gave him so much gentleness

and compassion.

From Kisi, Kenya

Kwamboka Okari sent the photo of the girls'
dorm

to Alice

with a note: Look what we have done with
some of the gift

from Yoko Ono and her husband (this made
Alice chuckle).

Alice was so happy she started to sing a song
that once

meant the world to her: Changing
the lyrics

only a little:

All we have is love;

All we have is love;

All we have is love, love;

Love is all we have.

And she felt so lucky to know in her heart

that this is a major moment of

enlightenment,

this awareness:

once again she gave thanks

to her new friend's father

who sang so many years ago

and with such gusto

that it's just as well that love is all we have

because love is all we need.

Alice and Sean Lennon

* * *

Alice and Kwamboka

This is Alice and Kwamboka
Sitting peaceful
on a sofa:
the green king
of blues
communing with Lucille
just
behind us![3]

✳ ✳ ✳

May It Be Said of Me

May it be said of me
That when I saw
Your mud hut
I remembered
My shack.
That when I tasted your
Pebble filled beans
I recalled
My salt pork.
That when I saw
Your twisted Limbs
I embraced
My wounded
Sight.
That when you
Rose from your knees
And stood
Like women
And men
Of this Earth—
As promised to us
As to anyone:
Without regrets

Of any kind
I joined you—
Singing.

* * *

And Do You See What They Have Bought with It?

You have bought
Foolish hats
From madmen
In Paris
You have bought
Shoes
You never
Intend to wear
You have
Bought
Cars for
Each day
Of
The week.

You ride
Faster than
Our donkeys
Can
Think;
Splashed with

The perfume
of our mothers'
Tears.

On
Television
You appear
In all your
Innocence

Wearing the spectacles
Whose frames
Our turtles
Unwillingly
Donated to you
With their
Shells

You speak
About our danger
To you

Our anger
And envy
And greed.

You are genuinely surprised to see us

Not only standing

But even more

Mysteriously

Armed, absolutely,

With the graceful

Power

Of speech.

But we were busy

In those shacks

&

Mud huts

Before dark;

Before the mosquitoes

Drove us

From our books.

We know

What you take

From us

And what

Useless things

—never love or peace or happiness—

You buy

With it.

* * *

She

For Gloria Steinem

She is the one
who will notice
that the first snapdragon
of Spring
is
in bloom;

She is the one
who will tell the most
funny
&
complicated
joke.

She is the one
who will surprise you
by knowing the difference
between turnips
and collard
Greens;

& between biscuits
& scones.

She is the one who knows where
to take you
for dancing
or where the food
& the restaurant's
décor
are not
to be
missed.

She is the one
who is saintly.

She is the one
who reserves the right
to dress
like a slut.

She is the one
who takes you shopping;

She is the one
who knows where

the best clothes
are bought
cheap.

She is the one
who warms your
home
with her fragrance;

the one who brings
music, magic & joy.

She is the one
Speaking
the truth
from her heart.

She is the one at the bedside
wedding, funeral
or divorce
of all the best people
you dearly love.

She is the one
with courage.

She is the one
who speaks
her bright mind;

She is the one
who encourages young &
old
to do the same.

She is the one
on the picket line, at the barricade,
at the prison, in jail;

She is the one
who is there.

If they come for me
& I am at her house
I know
she will hide me.

If I tell her
where I have hidden
my heart
she will keep

my secret
safe.

She is the one
who
without hesitation
comes to my aid &
my defense.

She is the one
who believes
my side of the story
first;

She is the one
whose heart
is open.

She is the one who loves.

She is the one who makes
activism
the most compelling
because she is the one
who is irresistible
her own self.

She is our sister, our teacher, our friend:
Gloria Steinem.

Born 75 years ago
Glorious
To your parents
& still
Radiant
Today.

Happy Birthday, Beloved.
The grand feast
Of your noble Spirit
Has been
& is the cake
that nourishes
Us.

We thank you for your Beauty
& your Being.

Namaste.[4]

* * *

Our Martyrs

For the Egyptian people

When the people
have won a victory
whether small
or large
do you ever wonder
at that moment
where the martyrs
might be?
They who sacrificed
Themselves
to bring to life
something unknown
though nonetheless more precious
than their blood.
I like to think of them
hovering over us
wherever we have gathered
to weep and to rejoice;
smiling and laughing,
actually slapping each other's palms
in glee.

Their blood has dried
and become rose petals.
What you feel brushing your cheek
is not only your tears
but these.

Martyrs never regret
what they have done
having done it.
Amazing too
they never frown.
It is all so mysterious
the way they remain
above us
beside us
within us;
how they beam
a human sunrise
and are so proud.

*   *   *

The tree of life has fallen

For the departing dictator, in perpetuity

The tree of life
has fallen on my small house.
I thought it was so much bigger!
But it is not.
There in the distance I see the mountains
still.
The view of vast water stretching before me
is superb.
My boat is grand and I still command the
    captain
of it; not having learned myself to sail.
But I am adrift
without my tree of life
that has fallen heavy
without grace or pity
on this small place.

*   *   *

To Change the World Enough

To change the world enough
you must cease to be afraid
of the poor.
We experience your fear as the least
    pardonable of
humiliations; in the past
it has sent us scurrying off
daunted and ashamed
into the shadows.
Now,
the world ending
the only one all of us have known
we seek the same
fresh light
you do:
the same high place
and ample table.
The poor always believe
there is room enough
for all of us;
the very rich never seem to have heard
of this.
In us there is wisdom of how to share

loaves and fishes
however few;
we do this every day.
Learn from us,
we ask you.

We enter now
the dreaded location
of Earth's reckoning;
no longer far
off
or hidden in books
that claim to disclose
revelations;
it is here.
We must walk together without fear.
There is no path without us.

*   *   *

Blessed Are the Poor in Spirit

"Blessed are the poor in spirit (*for theirs is the
    kingdom of heaven*)."
Did you ever understand this?
If my spirit was poor, how could I enter heaven?
Was I depressed?
Understanding editing,
I see how a comma, removed or inserted
with careful plan,
can change everything.
I was reminded of this
when a poor young man
in Tunisia
desperate to live
and humiliated for trying
set himself ablaze;
I felt uncomfortably warm
as if scalded by his shame.
I do not have to sell vegetables from a cart as he
    did
or live in narrow rooms too small for spacious
    thought;
and, at this late date,
I do not worry that someone will

remove every single opportunity

for me to thrive.

Still, I am connected to, inseparable from,

this young man.

Blessed are the poor, in spirit, for theirs is the
  kingdom of heaven.

Jesus. (Commas restored).

Jesus was as usual talking about solidarity:
  about how we join with others

and, in spirit, feel the world, and suffering,
  the same as them.

This is the kingdom of owning the other as
  self, the self as other—

that transforms grief into

peace and delight.

I, and you, might enter the heaven

of right here

through this door.

In this spirit, knowing we are blessed,

we might remain poor.

* * *

What do I get for getting old? A Picture Story for the Curious!
(You supply the pictures!)

I get to meditate
in a chair!
Or against the wall
with my legs
stretched out!
(Or even in bed!)
I get to see
maybe half
of what I'm looking at!
(This changes everything!)
I get to dance
like the tipsy old men
I adored
when I was an infant!
(They never dropped me!)
I get to spend time with myself
whenever I want!
I get to ride a bicycle
with tall
handlebars!

(My posture improves!)
I get to give up
learning to sail!
I get to know
I will never speak
German!

I get to snuggle all
Morning
with my snuggler
of choice:
counting the hours
by how many times
we get up
to pee!
I get to spend time with myself
whenever I want!

I get to eat chocolate
with my salad.
Or even as a first course!
I get to forget!
I get to paint
with colors
I mix myself!

Colors
I've never seen
before.
I get to sleep
with my dog
& pray never to outlive
my cat!
I get to play
music
without reading
a note!
I get to spend time with myself
whenever I want!

I get to sleep
in a
hammock
under the same
stars
wherever I am!
I get to spend time with myself
whenever I want!

I get to laugh
at all the things

I don't know
& cannot
find!

I get to greet
people I don't remember
as if I know them
very well.
After all, how different
can they be?
I get to grow
my entire
garden
in a few
pots!
I get to spend time with myself
whenever I want!

I get to see
& feel
the suffering
of the whole
world
& to take
a nap

when I feel
like it
anyway!

I get to spend time with myself
whenever I want!

I get to feel
more love
than I ever thought
existed!
Everything appears to be made
of the stuff!
I feel this
especially for You! Though I may not
    remember
exactly which You
you are!
How cool is this!
Still, I get to spend time with myself
whenever I want!
And that is just a taste
as the old people used to say
down in Georgia
when I was a child

of what you get
for getting old.

Reminding us, as they witnessed our curiosity
about them, that no matter the losses, there's
something fabulous going on at every stage
of Life, something to let go of, maybe, but for
darn sure, something to get!

* * *

Desire

My desire
is always the same; wherever Life
deposits me:
I want to stick my toe
& soon my whole body
into the water.
I want to shake out a fat broom
& sweep dried leaves
bruised blossoms
dead insects
& dust.
I want to grow
something.
It seems impossible that desire
can sometimes transform into devotion;
but this has happened.
And that is how I've survived:
how the hole
I carefully tended
in the garden of my heart
grew a heart
to fill it.

* * *

March Births

Many brave souls
who inhabit my heart
entered the brightening
but still chilly door
of earthly Life in the changeable month
of March.

The deep, noble, easily bruised
Pisceans

Flowers
Themselves

Arrived in that part of the month
when hardly one white or lavender
crocus, daring, vulnerable
& sweet
can be found;
except perhaps
in the prescient
South.

And those others:

the late in the month
born
Ariesians—
Dragons
And butterflies—
Who were born
it seems
to set this world
of shyness
& daffodils
stunningly
on fire.

It was my destiny
to behold and to cherish
you all.

What these births
at winter's end
teach us to believe
is that what looks
frozen or even dead
may burst into bloom
unexpectedly
at any time.

That to love
another,
any other, is to align oneself
with eternal spring.

It is in fact
Loving
any other being
all one ever needs
one's self
To come to bud
& flower
once more
& be born
Again.[5]

*　*　*

Two boys on a pink tricycle

Sometimes we fall in love
With a people
For reasons
They might never know.
For instance,
In Dharamsala
In the foothills of
The Himalayas
We met a beautiful man
Whose life
Was children.
How to find them,
Feed them,
Ferry them across
The mountains
In the snow.

There were many
Who were motherless
But everywhere
All around their new home
Was cleanliness

Colorfulness
And light.

Two boys on a pink tricycle
Caught my heart
And then a little girl
Born to boss
The world someday
Strode by
All two and a half years
Of her.

Our friend, her guardian,
Smiled at my delight.

These children he said
Come to us over the mountains
Sometimes their parents
Die along the way.

Sometimes
These are the children
Of lovers
Who have met in sorrow
And surprise

Along the route
Away from home
On the path that leads
To a new life
They have no real idea
About.

These are the children
Created by the love
That can flourish
In the oddest of situations
The strangest
Of places.

We know they bring with them
Their parents' courage
Their bravery
In the face
Of every kind of threat.

That they are special
And destined to be
Grown-up and if at all possible
Happy and connected
To who their parents were

Is well known
To us.

* * *

Coming to Worship the
1,000-Year-Old Cherry Tree

Life is good. Goodness is its character;
all else is defamation.
The Earth is good. Goodness is its nature.

Nature is good. Goodness is its essence.

People are also good. Goodness is our offering;
our predictable yet unfathomable flowering.

Thankful and encouraged
Infused with our peaceful inheritance
May we not despair.

* * *

Listening to Bedouins, Thinking of Bob

Sometimes I look at your photograph
And I wonder: where did your smile go
When you died;
Where could such a sunrise hide?
Is it still out there among the foliage and the
     hills
The trees and the grass?
I believe it is there.
That we will find it waiting
To ferry us
On those days our hearts are heavy
with the pain of this world
And our own tears are the deep river
We must cross.

*   *   *

Peonies

For Oprah Winfrey

Years ago you sent me peonies
too many to actually count
in a green glass vase
so huge
that it reminded me of the sea.
You must have discerned
through my incessant
word droppings
—compost for my life—
how much I treasure them:
more than food itself,
when I was young.

And did you also know this flower
the peony
is one of few that requires
the help of others
in order to bloom?
That its indispensable friend
is the tiny ant

who, drawn to its sweetness,
opens it up?
Each and every Springtime
it does this.
Walking today
I thought of this solidarity, and of you, as I
    turned
toward home.

I wanted to praise all that you have given
us.
I was going to start by mentioning
Hatshepsut, the queen who ruled
Ancient Egypt
as king of all the lands.
But then realized
something closer to home and even more
    eternal:
You are the peony, sister;
you are also the ant.
We thank you for biting through your
own restrictions
and blooming
so fearlessly
all these years,

affirming in brilliant color and sound
our own need to open

and helping us out.

* * *

Black and White Cows

When you were little I delighted
in every word you uttered.
You were so clever!
For instance: the word "utter."
Holding your small hand to my throat
to feel why the word "utter" is so different
from the word "bark"
you wondered aloud:
So is it the same with cows?
You know, do cows
have them. Utters?

No, I said
udder is different
it is something
that carries milk.
You liked milk
especially chocolate.

Oh, you said, getting it
right away:
Utter I speak!
Udder I drink!

Close enough
I said,
adoring you.
We spent the morning
quietly sipping mugs of dark cocoa
smiling a lot
drawing & then painting
black and white cows.

* * *

Worms Won't Need a Menu

For my "girls"

I am glad
You will never
See
Menus
All over
The world
On which
Your flesh
Appears
In thousands
Of
Seductive
ways.

I console
Myself: Worms
Won't need
A menu
To describe
Their human
Dinners.

Still,

I like to imagine

Them

Sitting alert

At table

Reading

Of

Our

Succulence.

* * *

From Paradise to Paradise

From paradise
to paradise
I go
sweeping;
collecting
rocks
&
views;
owning
nothing
but what I feel.

Who taught
me this?
This thankfulness?

You did.
Maker of all
Paradises.

Without borders
or cessation.

Bowing
as
I kneel.

* * *

Sailing the Hot Streets of Athens, Greece

It has been so
hot!
Is it hot
where you are?
Penned up
in a destroyed
place?
In Gaza?

The whole world
distracted
by its weathers
& other
disasters
still is watching
us,
Gaza,
as we yearn
towards each other.

Trying to embrace
each other

to give each
other,
to ourselves
united,
a simple
hug.

The whole world
is watching
Gaza
& it is
wondering how
things
will
turn out.

They are making
it hard
for us to move
Gaza
& sometimes
we are
in despair
but I remind
us
that you

of all people
understand
obstruction.

They know this place
we are in, I say,
of not
being able to move.
They know it
intimately.
This place of stalemate
& stagnation, so unbearable
to any heart
that's free
is where they
hourly
live.

They will forgive
us
if we do not
arrive
on time.

Furthermore,
having left our

own homes

we are

already

there.

I believe

with all my heart

in the magic

and the power

of intention.

The women & men

with cameras

come

to record

our dreams

& our frustrations;

most of them are

young

& we are glad

of this.

We want them

to see their

counterparts

& their elders

attempting to make

this voyage

to endure

this crossing.

We pray they

are of good heart

& balanced

mind.

Even

the spies

among them

we hope

will learn

something

they may never

have guessed

before:

That a boat

filled

with love letters

from children

is a threat

to those

with

apparently
little memory
of youth
or experience
of love.

I have given
my word that I would
sail
and so I do—if not
on our boat
that is not so far
allowed to go
to sea,
then through
the air sending
thoughts and feelings
I sail:
We all sail.
We sail the hot, sticky
streets
of Athens, Greece
longing to see
the faces
& deliver

love letters

to the people

of Gaza.

*   *   *

Written on our beautiful boat whose canopy is a giant peaceful American flag, as we sailed the waters off the coast of Greece and were intercepted by armed commandos of the Greek coast guard.

Life Takes Its Own Sweet Time

Life takes
its own
sweet time
to configure
just the wound
to stagger us:
so we may never forget
who runs the show
in these territories.

For years
we may circle
the puncture
soundlessly
running mental fingers
around its edges
as if fearing
a drain
that might suck away
the soul.

A decade might pass
in silence

before we once again

test our timid

voice

to shout inside the wound

& discover

the miracle:

that where pain has lived

so resplendently

for so long

there now resides

an insouciant

exuberance

to match

our

newly revealed

and

irrepressible smile.

✳   ✳   ✳

One Meaning of the Immaculate Heart

To hate no one
& nothing:
this is one meaning
of the "immaculate
heart"
that I did not understand
before.
To see
every human
blunder
no matter
how stinking
as an odious
misuse
of God.

*   *   *

To Stand Beaming and Clapping

To stand beaming and clapping for anyone
who bombs water
& denies to children
its purity to drink
endangers you,
made mostly of water
as you are.
See this. Before it is too late.

* * *

And in that sacred time

For h. e.

And in that sacred time
as we quietly awaited our fate
we spoke of offspring
who have discovered
so much to resist bearing
in us.
Well, we might have said
if we had thought
of it;
as we
watched
through a porthole
of our boat
black booted
boarders
with guns
make
a starboard
approach:

there are children

who've never heard
about our
misadventures

or in any case
not all of them:

(we would offer full disclosure if they might ask):
waiting
to see
and perhaps understand our failures

for themselves
on the bombed

and barricaded beach

still so far away

in Gaza.

* * *

Why Peace Is Always a Good Idea

For Jacqui Hairston, with love

Because you could plant peach trees
And because of peace
You could eat them in five or six
Years

Peaches not trees

And your children
Could eat them
After you are gone!

And because you could not see
A friend for a long, long time
But
Because there is peace
You would not lose them forever
But see them next time they come
To town!

You could go ice skating
Or roller skating

And no guns would go off
Scaring you.

You could grow old
And have a nice long beard
And no rockets
Would appear
To set fire
To it!

You could swim in the ocean
And see turtles
And whales
And nothing would interrupt
You, even if you fell asleep
On your back!

Not a single bomb
Would be going off
Anywhere!
And people would let you drift
To shore
And then they'd wake
You
With music and some food
That

Would be strange to you
But so delicious!

They'd want you
To like their peaceful land:
They'd want to learn about yours.
Peace is great for this sort of thing.
And when you went home
There would be a whole house
Intact
Waiting for you.
Your room warm and cozy
And your dog happy to see you
And everything! Even the cat
Might take a look at you,
Seriously,
As if she cared!

All this can happen in peace.
Never in war.

And that is why Peace is *always* a good idea.
Earth likes it too! She's tired of being
    marched on and hit by crazy humans
Who never see how sweet she is
Or appreciate

Her windstorms
or
Her curves.

* * *

Hope

Hope never
to covet
the neighbors' house
with the fragrant
garden
from which a family
has been
driven by your soldiers;
mother, father,
grandparents,
the toddler and
the dog
now homeless:
huddled, holding on
to each other,
stunned
and friendless
beneath you
in the street:
sitting on
cobblestones
as if on the sofas
inside

that you have decided
to clean, recover and
keep.

Hope never
to say yes
to their misery.

Hope never to gaze
down into their faces
from what used to be
their rooftop.

Hope never to believe
this robbery
will make you a better
citizen of your new
country
as you unfurl and wave
its recent
flag
that has been given
to assure you
of this impossibility.

*   *   *

Tranquil

15 years (!)
have passed
since you gave us
the wicker
picnic basket
a gift
you said
to
Our Romance!
Today
I took it out
to use
for the first time
marveling at its crisp
readiness
after all
these years.
I washed
the two white plates
with their plain
blue trim
and dusted the glasses
knives and forks

and ran the still shiny

bottle opener

along my sleeve.

I unwrapped the candle.

What dreamers we were!

And how the Universe

opened itself up

to us.

Every moment

we were not stressed

our hearts jumping

and shouting

for joy.

Those times

are long gone

now

and I do not long

for them anymore.

Life has continued—

filled

with companion travelers

to the stars

and I

thumb out

to the wind

always manage

to catch

a ride.

I shake out

the blue and white

tablecloth and napkins—

to adorn the pond side

table

of a simple cook-out

with neighbors

and their boys

from down

the hill.

Happiness—

with its gaggle of chickens, ducks and dogs—

floods the scene.

Still,

Those were the days!

I think,

gloating

over the Dance of Life

—and our part in it—

already done.

I see

for an instant

your bright eyes

and merry smile

and savor

the sweet, sweet music

of memory

that resides

all these years

later

in a still

charmed

and tranquil

heart.

* * *

The Raping of Maids

Alas,
you do not know
who your fathers are:
they are the very reason
you felt queasy
not wanting the little girl
on the bus
to sit next to you.
There she was
in all her home-made
finery,
her hair curly, but with a similar
drift
to yours.
Her eyes
the ones you see
briefly
if he is home
at breakfast.
The history
of this assault is long
and so is memory
among the poor.

When you see your nanny

attempt to rise

at last

go to her defense.

You can do it now

you are not a child

helpless

as you were

for too long

to help

her stand.

* * *

This Human Journey

Don't waste one moment
Trying to be someone
different
or someplace other
than where
you are.

This human journey
is like
finding yourself
in Brussels
rather than
in Broccoli.

Find out what's good
about the place
—in Brussels
as in Broccoli—
there must be something.

*　*　*

In This You Are Wrong

In this
you are wrong.
Killing the prophet
will not make
you right.
Her blood sent flying
in all directions
by your assault
will become
innumerable seeds
that sprout
blades of bright grass
announcing the truth
like flags.
Killing the prophet
today
means
what it always has:
wandering the desert
of missed opportunity
lost
for another 1000 years.

* * *

Hope to Sin Only in the Service of Waking Up

Hope
never to believe
it is your duty
or right
to harm
another
simply because
you mistakenly believe
they are not you.

Hope
to understand
suffering
as the hard assignment
even in school
you wished
to avoid. But
could not.

Hope
to be imperfect
in all the ways

that keep you
growing.

Hope
never to see
another
not even a blade of grass
that is beyond your joy.

Hope
not to be a snob
the very day
Love
shows up
in love's
work clothes.

Hope to see
your own skin
in the wood
grains
of your house.

Hope
to talk
to trees

& at last
tell them everything
you've always
thought.

Hope
at the end
to enter
the Unknown
knowing
yourself. Forgetting
yourself
also.

Hope to be consumed
to disappear
into your own
Love.

Hope to know
where you are
—Paradise—
if nobody else
does.

Hope
that every failure
is an arrow
pointing toward
enlightenment.

Hope to sin
only
in the service
of waking up.

*   *   *

The Part of God That Stings

I am in agreement with the Buddha:

that these are natural

perhaps inevitable

human states; that spiritual retreats

though invaluable

are not essential

to their

achievement.

One day it will simply become

crystal clear

that all creatures

younger than us

are

our children;

just as all creatures

and entities

older than us

trees

and oceans

included

are our parents.

Amma

the hugging saint from Kerala

has put

this beautifully:

She speaks of this awareness

of being Mother

of all

while being Mothered

by all

as Divine Love.

As God.

One day

perhaps while sitting blankly

before a leaping fire

at home

or even while stalled in traffic

on the freeway

you will realize

that all creatures

when they enter

your house

are guests

regardless

of whether

they frighten you:

the ant, the gecko,

the cockroach,

the bat;
and that you are a guest
also
in their
much larger
home.
Mutual respect
though this seldom means
no killing
or cursing at all
is due.
There will seem to be
a few exceptions
but surely
this is illusion
as so much is!

For instance:
scorpions, vipers, and yellow jackets
in paradise?
How to accept
gracefully
the part of God
that stings!

* * *

9/11: An Irrelevant Truth

They tell so many lies
I do not wonder that you have lost trust
in human beings.

Now you ask me seriously:
Auntie, do those who tell humongous lies,
and get away with it, celebrate their victories
    the same
as those who tell, and get away with,
smaller, "whiter" ones?
Is it just a matter of bigger bottles
of champagne,
more expensive party girls
and a bigger cake?

What can I tell you?

Never believe "the truth" as set before you
by your enemies,
is about all I would say.
Be alert to whatever makes no sense
to you.

You are an expert, no matter how much they
    tell you
that you are not.
You know some things fall down
crooked and some things
fall down
in a straight line:
I am not speaking of your parents, but there too
you've had experience.

Humans,
with all of our experience of it
find absolute evil almost impossible
to believe. Even looking at it.
We will stand around
shot through
the eye
and the heart
and never notice we are being
bled to death.

That is why I feel this tenderness
this overwhelming
tenderness
for the human race:
we are so gullible and so trusting

and so afraid by now: we are willing to believe
anything;
even that Truth itself is irrelevant
if the lie is big enough.

* * *

The Buddha's Disagreeable Relative

Even the Buddha, the Enlightened one,
had a disagreeable relative.
I learned this while on retreat
in the homeland of
notable tough relatives:
the state of Texas
U.S.A.
Although it doesn't really matter
where we learn
the bit of news that helps us.
We are grateful!
I think I learned he was a cousin, maybe a
    nephew
of Gautama
but anyhow
he hated Buddha.
Lied about him, made up stories,
stole Buddha's stuff: one of his cloaks, his best
    begging bowl, maybe, or a couple
of his walking sticks.
How much stuff does a Buddha own,
after all?

Why should the Buddha of all people
even need a disagreeable relative?
our teacher asked.
He was from Harvard University
in New England
where there are
as many notable disagreeable relatives
as in Texas
and where one imagines
talk of the Buddha
must take many an elegant academic twist
    and evasive turn.
But to the sufferer in the trenches
of familial acrimony
and abuse
the only answer
must be this:
no one is exempt
and certainly not a Buddha
from the need to balance
enlightenment
with the
head bowing despair
of daily practice.

* * *

We Who Have Survived

For Troy Davis

Though they elicit
yawns
from our friends
we who have survived
fierce battle
must tell our war stories
over and over
again.
Our tale is like a lost
coin
re-found
when we are starving
shining with new power
of purchase
as
fresh light strikes:
token of our
deliverance.

* * *

Racism Dates Us
(Speciesism does too)

For Troy Davis

Racism dates us
(Speciesism does too).
I know we don't care;
it feels so good
to feel
superior
to other beings
for reasons
they do not control.

There we go
talking about the blacks
the browns
the reds
the yellows
and the whites
as if our children
haven't already painted
and repainted

God's face (adding a tattoo—and a feather—
   here and there)

and returned it
glowing
to Her cosmic
coloring box.

*   *   *

The World We Want Is Us

It moves my heart to see your awakened faces;
the look of "aha!"
shining, finally, in
so many
wide open eyes.
Yes, we are the 99%
all of us
refusing to forget
each other
no matter, in our hunger, what crumbs
are dropped by
the 1%.
The world we want is on the way; Arundhati
and now we
are
hearing her breathing.
The world we want is Us; *united*; already moving
into it.

* * *

The Joyful News of Your Arrest

this sunday morning everything
is bringing tears.
in church this morning
not a church anyone from my childhood
would
recognize
as church
a brother singing
ecstatic
about the bigness of love
and then this moment
news of your arrest
on the steps of the supreme court
a place of intrigue and distrust;
news of the illegal sign you carried
that you probably made yourself:
Poverty Is the Greatest Violence of All.
brother cornel. brother west.
what a joy it is
to hear this news of you.
that you have not forgotten
what our best people taught us
as they rose to meet their day:

not to be silent

not to fade into the shadows

not to live and die in vain.

But to glorify

the love that demands

we stand

in danger

shaking off

our chains.

*   *   *

Every Revolution Needs
Fresh Poems

Every revolution needs fresh poems
that is the reason
poetry cannot die.
It is the reason poets
go without sleep
and sometimes without lovers
without new cars
and without fine clothes
the reason we commit
to facing the dark
and
resign ourselves, regularly, to the possibility
of being wrong.
Poetry is leading us.
It never cares how we will
be held by lovers
or drive fast
or look good
in the moment;
but about how completely
we are committed
to movement

both inner and outer;
and devoted to transformation
and to change.

* * *

The Foolishness of Captivity
An Open Poem for Who the Shoe Fit

Younger brother,
it is plain as day to those who love you
that you have fallen into the devil's hands.
It can happen, all too easily, to good people;
look at Jesus: He fell and has kept falling
for over two thousand years;
that is how they keep him
pacified and pale and nailed
to that cross.

How to escape?

First, admit whose hands
you have fallen into:
admit how pleased you were
when you finally
arrived there.
Devils have limos and fine
china to offer;
carpeting made by elves
and all manner of sleek
hovercraft.

You were so poor!

Next, watch carefully
with one eye open
even while asleep
to discover
how much blood
your favorite devil is sucking
from you.

Listen, please, to the old women
in your life.
This same devil held them down
for eons
burning them with pleasure
for his devilish advancement,
any time he needed to.
But really they,
like the devil, himself,
appear to be
Indestructible;
though I could be wrong.

The point is: learn to hear something
besides your own voice.

It doesn't seem to belong to you
anymore. It is his. It is hers.

I see, as you must,
the vampires
who have "succeeded"
playing the devil's game.
They are all over the
talk shows now;
fresh blood absorbed,
beakers of it
from around the globe,
they have become plump
and disturbingly shiny.

Perhaps this bloated look
of satisfaction,
of hastily devoured "enemies"
is one to which you aspire?
Like a Botox fix
though,
it isn't lasting, little brother,
I can assure you.

Wake up!
Ruling the earth

is not the fun
it might have seemed.
How many butterflies
do you get to notice
on a regular basis
& write haiku
about?
And do you even know
where they've stashed
your kayak
and
your bike?
It is not too late
to transform!

Remember Milarepa?
The murderer who turned into a poet and a saint?
I like to. He cures my every desire
to be perfect and never bad.
"Murderer. Magician. Saint." That is how
among certain Buddhists
he is described. There is a film about him
by a director from Bhutan. You should watch it
to see how far you can fall
and still get back up. Though not back up
into the same location. *Please.*

He too fell into the devil's
hands. Hands attached to his mother's
grief, in his case,
and memories of his own mistreatment,
by greedy neighbors and selfish relatives, as a boy.
He was so angry,
he destroyed his whole village!
People he knew intimately. Which might be worse
than destroying a whole village
of people you don't know;
a problem you could have.

Of course they were
terrorists
(who made his childhood hell)
but what of his own
soul, even so?

Whenever you wake up
and find yourself
in the devil's hands
there is always something you can do:
usually it is the thing we think of first: so of course
we dismiss it right away!

You can jump out.
And that is my advice.

Jump
out quickly. Take only your wife,
your children, your animals and other
kin. Grab your umbrella, too,
and flee.
Trust me, there is no shame
in this. Only sanity
and
soul preservation.
It's a smart move.

Not everyone has the good sense
to resign
to quit the devil's employment.
To see through the silky
carpet underfoot at
the Commander's desk
to the dirt floor
beneath;
under which there are
so many buried things.

Besides,

working for the devil (temporarily)

is sometimes, curiously, a necessity

for future growth.

There can be, after many disasters,

a bit of progression!

Milarepa, again.

"Murderer. Magician. Saint."

Listen:

Go to the forest. Get lost there. Find a shack to

live in. A shack that, like your soul, might need

endless days and nights of repair. Let your

hair grow out. Your soul reviving, you'll look

great with locks!

In any case: Disappear from the devil's

  plantation;

let him harvest his own poisoned crops.

It's just a job. This charade called ruling.

A thankless one, at that.

There is life, so much life

beyond the stressful "glamour"

of the devil's hands.

Or, Come to the caves
that open
to the wind
above the blue
and
ceaseless counsel of the sea.
Weren't you born
within the sound
of deep water?

Some of us, coming back
from our own
lethal employments
can meet you there:
we can bring drums, guitars,
tambourines and flutes.
A singing bowl!
We can bring backpacks filled
with medicine
and stories from the ancestors
about
how they escaped
from the foolishness
of captivity;
to make the long journey back

to peace;
to The Beloved
and to the soul.

＊　＊　＊

My own definition of "the devil": *In human affairs
it is the force that operates without empathy.*
Also:
"The Beloved": *whatever one feels as* "God."
"Peace": *the fruit of justice done especially to the
Self.*
"Soul": *all that one has, ultimately, as guide and
deliverer.*

Despair Is the Ground Bounced Back From

When the best mothering
you can muster
is kicked to the curb
with a sneer;
when the best fathering
you have in you
to provide
is banished
and ridiculed;
there is still something
to be gained
to be learned
to be
absorbed
even in this pit.
Despair is the ground
bounced back
from:
How else are we to learn
intimately
the pain
of Mother Earth

the deep sorrow
of Father Sky.
Giving their all
every second
to all they engender
together.
Not one minute
in all Eternity
bereft of their
best
effort.
Yet kicked
with disdain
to the curb of human
relevance;
as humans
orphaned now
drift
in meaningless
tantrum
bereft not only
of parents
but of a future.

*   *   *

Occupying Mumia's Cell

I Sing of Mumia
brilliant and strong
and of the captivity
that
few black men escape
if they are as free
as he has become.

What a teacher he is for all of us.

Nearly thirty years in solitary
and still,
Himself.

He will die himself.
A black man;
whom many consider to be
a Muslim, though this is not
how he narrows down
the criss-crossing paths of
his soul's journey.
Perhaps it is simpler
to call him

a lover of truth

who refuses

to be silenced.

Is anything more persecuted

in this land?

No boots will be allowed

of course

so he will not

die with them on;

but there will always be

boots

of the mind and spirit

and of the heart and soul.

His will be black and shining

(or maybe the color of rainbows)

and they will sprout wings.

Mumia

they have decided

finally

not to kill you

hoping no blood will

stain their hands

at the tribunal

of the people;
but to let you continue
to die slowly
creating and singing
your own songs
as you pace
alone, sometimes terrorized,
for decades of long nights
in your small cage
of a cell.
We lament our impotence: that we have failed
to get you out of there.

Your regal mane may have thinned
as our locks too, those flags of our self
    sovereignty, may even have
disappeared;
waiting out this unjust sentence,
until we, like you, have become old.
Still,
if you will: accept our gratitude
that you stand, even bootless,
on your feet. We see
that few of those around us,
well shod and walking, even owning, the streets
are freed.

Somehow you have been.

Enough to remind us
of freedom's devout
internal and
ineradicable seed.

What a magnificent Lion
you have been all these
disastrous years
and still are,
indeed.

*   *   *

Another Way to Peace

It is compelling to watch
the few
still free
of it.
Who were never caged
within the false bright light
of "the set"
nor ever pinned to the couch
by TV.

Interviewed by a mannequin
they do not seem to notice
the silent eye
watching them;
training them to sit just so
or it will enlarge
their noses
flatten their foreheads
screw up their color
or otherwise
be displeased.

They sit with legs
stretched out.
They yawn.

They rub their cheeks:
make-up be damned.
If they find a piece of lint
on trousers or skirt
they might examine it.

To the TV trained
they must appear
to be from a place
never experienced:
where people do not freeze
when talking to strangers.

A place where it is ok
to look at the sky—before answering
a silly
question—
as if asking the Gods
for help.

Ok to blow one's nose.

To be free, uncaged,
after years of disobeying,
of ignoring,
television
is another way to peace.

To sink back
quietly
into the unclipped
vegetation of regular Life
where we —despite
the blared stimulation
of incessant programming—
can rest content
to simply be.

* * *

We Pay a Visit to Those Who Play at Being Dead

For Rudolph, Beverly, Henri, Alice,
Garrett, Angel, Pratibha, Kiietti, Arbie

My mother
For instance
Whose
Cheekbones
Greet me
From
A
Recent
Photograph
Of myself.

My father:
Those eyes
In the
Mirror
I would
Recognize
Anywhere.

My brother's

Tree,

That he planted

Years

Before

He

Was

Planted

Himself,

Is awash

In light

Robustly

Proclaiming

His

Vivid

If

Persistently

Mysterious

Presence.

My grandparents

Henry

& Rachel

Whose voices

Are

Perpetually

Murmuring
Sweet nothings
In my
Heart.

Look!
I say to all
Of them:
The cousins
&
The
Outside
Children
Too—
I have
Brought
Friends!

We sit
Content
&
Munch
Our
Veggie salad
& Forbidden
Potato

Chips
Sitting
Serene
Amongst
Your graves.

You are silent.

A granddaughter
My niece
Who cares
That your
Graves
Are kept
Clean
As she
Has always
Known
Them,
Lowers
Her
Shapely
Form
To rest
On an Army Veteran's
Tombstone.

So many
Of you—
I had not noticed
This before—
Went off
To fight
Strangers.

Returning
Wounded
Dead
Or
Strangers
Yourselves.

You are quiet, too, as we sit
Munching
Our lunch.

But are
You really
Dead?

Are you not
Perhaps

The reason
I have no
Enthusiasm
Patience
Or admiration
For war?

You,
The
Poor
Dispossessed
Cannon
Fodder

Safer behind
The mule
You
Left
Than
Behind
Any
Gun?

My friend
Pratibha (her name means genius in her
Original language

Which is Hindu)

Brown

Indian

British

With

An accent

That

Would

Have

Made

You laugh

(as your own Southern country accent

Amused many)

Films

Us all

Sitting

Talking

Eating

Laughing

Being with

You,

As you

Play dead.

Later in

The van

Leaving

Your place

Of enchanted

Rest

We marvel

At who

Life

Has put into

Our vehicle.

Old friends

By now

Really

Because

Of you.

There is

No other

Explanation

Though

You

May

Continue

Your little
Afterlife game
Of
Playing dead.

* * *

Democratic Womanism

For Wongari Maathai

*Traditionally capable, as in: "Mama, I'm
walking to Canada, and I'm taking you
and a bunch of other slaves with me."
Reply: "It wouldn't be the first time."*

—from the definition of "Womanist" in
In Search of Our Mothers' Gardens:
Womanist Prose, *1983, by the author*

You ask me why I smile
when you tell me you intend
in the coming national elections

to hold your nose
and vote for the lesser of two evils.
There are more than two evils out there,
is one reason I smile.
Another is that our old buddy Nostradamus
comes to mind, with his dreadful
400-year-old prophecy: that our world
and theirs too
(our "enemies"— lots of kids included here)
will end (by nuclear nakba or holocaust)
in our lifetime. Which makes the idea of elections
and the billions of dollars wasted on them
somewhat fatuous.

A Southerner of Color,
my people held the vote
very dear
while others, for centuries,
merely appeared to play
with it.

One thing I can assure
you of is this:
I will never betray such pure hearts
by voting for evil
even if it were microscopic

which, as you can see in any newscast
no matter the slant,
it is not.

I want something else;
a different system
entirely.
One not seen
on this earth
for thousands of years. If ever.

Democratic Womanism.

Notice how this word has "man" right in the
  middle of it?
That's one reason I like it. He is there, front and
  center. But he is surrounded.

I want to vote and work for a way of life
that honors the feminine;
a way that acknowledges
the theft of the wisdom
female and dark Mother leadership
might have provided our spaceship
all along.

I am not thinking
of a talking head
kind of gal:
happy to be mixing
it up
with the baddest
bad boys
on the planet
her eyes a slit
her mouth a zipper.

No, I am speaking of true
regime change.
Where women rise
to take their place
en masse
at the helm
of earth's frail and failing ship;
where each thousand years
of our silence
is examined
with regret,
and the cruel manner in which our values
of compassion and kindness
have been ridiculed
and suppressed

brought to bear on the disaster
of the present time.

The past must be examined closely, I believe,
*   before we can leave*
it there.

I am thinking of Democratic, and, perhaps
Socialist, Womanism.
For who else knows so deeply
how to share but Mothers
and Grandmothers? Big sisters
and Aunts?
To love
and adore
both female and male?
Not to mention those in between.
To work at keeping
the entire community
fed, educated
and safe?

Democratic womanism,
Democratic Socialist
Womanism,
would have as its icons

such fierce warriors

for good as

Vandana Shiva

Aung San Suu Kyi,

Wangari Maathai

Harriet Tubman

Yoko Ono

Frida Kahlo

Angela Davis

Celia Sanchez

& Barbara Lee:

With new ones always rising, wherever you

look. Recent writers for instance:

Michelle Alexander, Isabel Wilkerson, and

Nancy Turner Banks, MD. Whose

books, read together, go a long way toward

bringing us up to speed on how our

declining country got this way.

You are also on this list, but it is so long (Isis

would appear midway) that I must stop or

be unable to finish the poem). So just know I've

stood you in a circle that includes

Marian Wright Edelman, Amy Goodman,

Sojourner Truth, Gloria Steinem and Mary

McLeod Bethune. John Brown, Frederick

Douglass, John Lennon and Howard Zinn
are there too. Happy to be surrounded!

There is no system
now in place
that can change
the disastrous course
Earth is on.

Who can doubt this?

The male leaders
of Earth
appear to have abandoned
their very senses
though most appear
to live now
entirely
in their heads.

They murder humans and other
animals
forests and rivers and mountains
every day
they are in office

and never seem
to notice it.

They eat and drink devastation.

Women of the world,
Is this devastation Us?
Would we kill whole continents for oil
(or anything else)
rather than limit
the number of consumer offspring we produce
and learn how to make our own fire?

Democratic Womanism.
Democratic Socialist Womanism.
A system of governance
we can dream and imagine and build together.
    One that recognizes
at least six thousand years
of brutally enforced complicity
in the assassination
of Mother Earth, but foresees six thousand years
ahead of us when we will not submit.

What will we need? A hundred years
at least to plan: (five hundred will be handed us

gladly

when the planet is scared enough)

in which circles of women meet,

organize ourselves, and,

allied with men

brave enough to stand with women,

nurture our planet to a degree of health.

And without apology—

(impossible to make

a bigger mess than has been made)—

devote ourselves, heedless of opposition,

to tirelessly serving and resuscitating Our

    Mother ship

and with gratitude

for Her care of us

worshipfully commit

to

rehabilitating it.

*   *   *

Democratic Motherism

My partner, a musician and Vietnam veteran
(virtually kidnapped and forced to serve in
that disastrous and genocidal war without his
consent), is someone brave enough to stand
with women, unafraid of being surrounded
by or led by them. In conversing about what
it will take to reclaim our planet we agreed
that what Earth needs more than anything
is mothering. Earth, Mother Earth, needs
mothers, regardless of gender—though we all
recognize who most mothers have been, and
are. Mothering is an instinct, yes, but it is also
a practice. It can be learned. For women it
has been an eons-long experience: the art and
necessity of taking care of all, of everything,
of mothering. So perhaps the new "ism" we
are talking about is not classic Womanism,
but Motherism. Democratic Motherism.

In any case, we will continue to endure,
and detest, the systems currently in place, in
which the condition of countless starving,
tortured, enslaved and murdered children
is seen as acceptable, unless we forthrightly

begin to envision, and work for, something better: some way for humans to exist and thrive, without suffering the despair of every second of every day knowing our present predicament's greatest cause is humanity's fear of sharing equally with others, and its rapidly growing, partly because of this fear, self-hatred.

On a recent visit to a still and quiet sacred site in Hawaii that is now surrounded by the pollution of unimaginable overcrowdedness and lack of peace, I recently experienced an insight that seemed at the time to be a direct message from ancestors who had used that site for thousands of years: it came to me in the form of the name for a new world political party (no kidding!). The Mother Defend Yourself Party. "Mother" referring to Earth. A poem (of course) accompanied it.

> Mother defend
> Yourself:
> We who love you
> Stand witness
> To
> Your innocence.

One of this party's first responsibilities would be to unite all segments of the globe in making offerings at the scene of every place the earth fights back in the effort to reclaim her freedom and integrity from the tyranny imposed on her by humanity. Where dams have burst, where forest fires have raged, where hillsides have crumbled. Where rivers have run wild. I am saying, as I believe, that we must begin again to have conversation with our planet.

It was in Hawaii on an earlier visit, again to a sacred site (although of course all of Hawaii is sacred), that this became even clearer to me.

A friend and I had gone on a "tour" of sorts that brought us to this place. We got out of the van and stood with our group at the designated "lookout" point. We were looking into a landscape that, though "beautiful" in the Kodak-moment sense, was lifeless and uninspiring. I commented on this to my Hawaiian friend, an artist, who shrugged and said: Of course. That is because what you're looking at, this whole area, was traditionally sung to. What? I said. Yes, she said. Where

we're standing used to be almost like a stage.
Folks who knew what they were doing,
praising the *aina* (the land), would come here
and sing their gratitude.

Well, I said. You are a singer. Sing!

Grabbing her tiny ukulele, which
accompanied her everywhere, she did just that.

As she sang in Hawaiian (a language
outlawed by U.S. colonial rule for decades; her
aunt had created a Hawaiian dictionary in an
effort to preserve the language) it seemed to
me the trees and other vegetation responded
by standing taller, fluffing themselves up. The
flowers among them appeared to fling their
scent. I became vividly aware of everything's
aliveness.

This token of gratitude, awareness, affection,
might be our party's first step.[6]

✳ ✳ ✳

After Many Years and Much Silliness

After many years
and much silliness on both our parts
I invite you back to this sacred place
we used to come
to rest, to sleep, to dream;
to heal
our brokenness.

I know you've missed it.

The *rosa morada* trees
whose blossoms consoled us
and the moonlit *maguey*
that made us wonder
were taken out by last month's hurricane.

I witness the bare spaces with your eyes. And
    wait,
humbled, for your murmurs of acceptance
and letting go.

We are adrift now. Every boat has left the shore.

Everything in Nature is warning us
to hurry up
and share.

*   *   *

When I Join You

When I join you
in the effort for peace
I give myself over.
There
and not there.
Marching
with you
alongside
the many who have died
it is as if we are marching
across the Universe
and just ahead of us
if only in another galaxy
there is a door.

*   *   *

Going Out to the Garden

Going out to the garden
this morning
to plant seeds
for my winter greens
—the strong, fiery mustard
& the milder
broadleaf turnip—
I saw a gecko
who
like the rest of us
has been reeling from the heat.

Geckos like heat
I know this
but the heat
these last few days
has been excessive
for us
& for them.

A spray of water
from the hose
touched its skin:

I thought it would
run away.
There are crevices
aplenty
to hide in:
the garden wall
is made of stones.

But no
not only
did the gecko
not run away
it appeared
to raise
its eyes
& head
looking for more.

I gave it.

Squirt after
squirt
of cooling
spray
from the green
garden hose.

Is it the end
of the world?
It seemed to ask.
This bliss,
is it Paradise?

I bathed it
until we were both
washed clean
of the troubles
of this world
at least for this moment:
this moment of pleasure
of gecko
joy
as I with so much happiness
played Goddess
to Gecko.

* * *

Notes

1. The poems of *The World Will Follow Joy: Turning Madness into Flowers* were written between October 2009 and August 2011.

2. Three deep bows to Noelle Hanrahan, Angela Davis and Gloria LaRiva. Champions of liberty; long distance, unwavering.

For a fuller comprehension of this poem please view these films: *Incident at Oglala*, *In Prison My Whole Life*, *Trudell*, and *Why We Fight*.

3. B. B. King and Lucille, his guitar.

4. April 20, 1997, New York City, the 92nd St. Y. Italicized portion of the poem written in September, 2009.

5. Happy Birthday, beloveds! Gloria, Quincy, Mel, Tracy, Flannery. And especially the March-born hero who started it all: my brother Bill. William Henry Walker. Born March 23, a smiling, generous, well-balanced baby and child who was the same as a man.

6. *The Warmth of Other Suns: The Epic Story of America's Great Migration*, by Isabel Wilkerson; *AIDS, Opium, Diamonds and Empire: The Deadly Virus of International Greed*, by Nancy Turner Banks, MD; and *The New Jim Crow: Mass Incarceration in the Age of Colorblindness*, by Michelle Alexander—these three books, read in this order, are a university course in history and present-day reality hard to obtain otherwise. Enjoy! Not because they're easy to read. They're not. They are deeply painful. The joy comes from their existence, since our only hope is knowing what is (and has been) going on.

Someone has said, "We don't need another 'ism'." And I agree that the "isms" of the past have been tiresome; but this is partly because woman, and especially dark woman, had no real place in them. In any event, this offering, like all those made now, is comparable to a simple discarded stone brought with humility to the collective pile of our understanding as we look the future in the face and resolve, whatever our fears, to move forward.

Photo Credits

Page 44: (top) New dormitory for the girls of Margaret Okari Primary School © Kwamboka K. Okari; (middle) Yvonne and Brenda © Kwamboka K. Okari; (bottom) Flower image courtesy of the Dale M. Mcdonald Collection, State Library and Archives of Florida.

Page 52: Alice Walker and Sean Lennon © Pratibha Parmar/Kali Films.

Page 53: Alice Walker with Kwamboka K. Okari, executive director of the Margaret Okari Children's Foundation © Kwamboka K. Okari

Page 67: Image of fallen tree courtesy of Laura Balandran.

Page 69: Image of path courtesy of FreeBigPictures.com.

Page 87: Image of Alice and others with picture of Bob Marley courtesy of L.A. Hyder, www.lahyderphotography.com.

Page 171: Wangari Maathai © Martin Rowe.

Page 189: Image of gecko by iStock.

CELEBRATING INDEPENDENT PUBLISHING

Thank you for reading this book published by The New Press. The New Press is a nonprofit, public interest publisher. New Press books and authors play a crucial role in sparking conversations about the key political and social issues of our day.

We hope you enjoyed this book and that you will stay in touch with The New Press. Here are a few ways to stay up to date with our books, events, and the issues we cover:

- Sign up at www.thenewpress.com/ subscribe to receive updates on New Press authors and issues and to be notified about local events
- Like us on Facebook: www.facebook. com/newpressbooks
- Follow us on Twitter: www.twitter.com/ thenewpress

Please consider buying New Press books for yourself; for friends and family; or to donate to schools, libraries, community centers, prison libraries, and other organizations involved with the issues our authors write about.

The New Press is a 501(c)(3) nonprofit organization. You can also support our work with a tax-deductible gift by visiting www. thenewpress.com/donate.